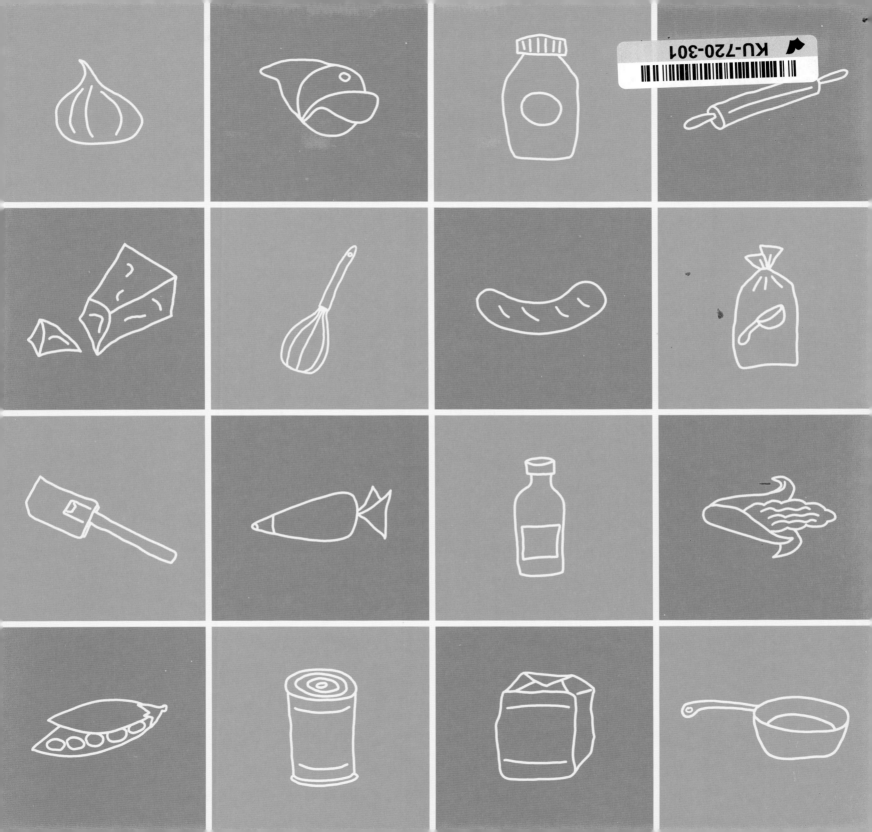

Cooking with Kids

Cooking with Kids

authors
Erin & Tatum Quon

photographer
David Matheson

WELDON
OWEN

contents

about this book

Cooking with your kids is a fun activity the whole family can enjoy together. This collection of easy-to-prepare, family-friendly recipes encourages creativity in the kitchen and teaches everyone—adults and kids alike—how easy it is to prepare delicious, healthy dishes with fresh ingredients. In the pages that follow, you will find new twists on old favourites, such as French toast bites with blueberry sauce and inside-out apple crisp, as well as classics like chicken potpie and ice cream bonbons. Colourful photos of yummy food and ideas on how to make fun variations will grab your kids' attention and have them eager to help.

TATUM QUON

getting started

Our lives are a lot busier and it's hard to find the time to teach our kids basic cooking skills that will help them as they grow. With inspiring recipes and dishes the whole family will love to make and eat, this book will help you get started doing just that. Here are some tips for keeping things fun in the kitchen:

Choose a recipe   Decide together what you want to make, then read through the recipe so there are no surprises.

Gather your ingredients   Get out all of the ingredients and tools you'll need for making the recipe.

Prepare your ingredients   Rinse and dry off fruits and vegetables before you use them. Handle delicate ingredients, like berries and tomatoes, gently. Give tough-skinned vegetables, like potatoes and carrots, a good scrub. It's also a good idea to measure everything out before you begin making the recipe.

Keep it safe   Adults should always stay in the kitchen to lend a hand when needed. Let kids know it's okay to ask questions as they work or to ask for help when needed.

Clean it up   Clear off and clean a space that's big enough to cook comfortably. Clean up work surfaces and tools as you use them, and wash your hands with warm water and soap before you handle anything. Being neat as you cook makes cleanup easier and cooking more fun.

using the recipes

The recipes in this cookery book are intended for kids ages 4–8, to use with as much independence as seems right for their age and skill level. Only you, the parents, can gauge how much support you will need to give your children as they cook. Help your children by reviewing the recipe with them before they begin and going over any questions they may have. To make this process easier, we have designed the recipes to identify the steps that kids can do on their own. These are our suggestions only, not strict requirements.

for parents

Each recipe contains steps which are meant for you, the parents, to take the lead on, like using knives for chopping, stirring on a hot stovetop, and putting things into and pulling them out of the oven. However, you know your children's skill levels best, so have them help out as much or as little as you feel comfortable.

for kids

 Every recipe in this book includes call outs for kids. Just look for the chef's hat and the orange text, review the step with your parent, and get started. If you need help, just ask. It's always better to be safe!

rise & shine

There are few better ways to rouse your little sleepyheads from their slumber than the promise of breakfast made together. Miniature pancakes with bananas. Crunchy home-made granola. Crisp cubes of cinnamon French toast ready for dipping. Morningtime goodies offer ample opportunity for even the smallest kids to accomplish much of the preparation themselves. Just pull a kitchen stool up to the counter and let the kids take charge.

breakfast pinwheels

 Large eggs 4

 Cheddar cheese
60g shredded

 Salt and pepper
Big pinch each

 Butter 30g

 Wholemeal tortillas
2 (15cm)

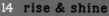 **Ham** 4 slices

Makes 2 servings

 In a bowl, whisk together the eggs and half of the cheese. Season with salt and pepper.

In a sauté pan over medium heat, melt half of the butter. Add the eggs and cook, stirring constantly with a spatula, until cooked through but still soft and moist, about 6 minutes. Remove from the heat, transfer to a bowl, and set aside.

 Lay the tortillas on a work surface. Scoop half of the scrambled eggs onto the top of each tortilla. Sprinkle the remaining cheese on top of the eggs, dividing it evenly between the tortillas. Top each tortilla with 2 slices of the ham. Working from the edge closest to you, roll up each tortilla.

Cut each rolled tortilla into 3 pieces. Pierce each piece with a toothpick to secure and serve.

waffles with strawberry sauce

Preheat a waffle iron. Preheat the oven to 120°C.

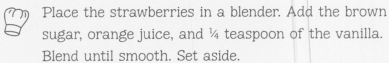 Place the strawberries in a blender. Add the brown sugar, orange juice, and ¼ teaspoon of the vanilla. Blend until smooth. Set aside.

In a large bowl, stir together the flour, granulated sugar, baking powder, and bicarbonate of soda. In another bowl, whisk together the buttermilk, milk, egg yolks, butter, and remaining ¼ teaspoon vanilla. Pour the buttermilk mixture into the flour mixture and stir until blended.

In a bowl, beat the egg whites using an electric mixer on medium speed until soft peaks form. Using a rubber spatula, fold the beaten egg whites into the flour-buttermilk mixture just until combined.

Lightly grease the waffle iron and ladle in enough batter for 1 waffle. Close the lid of the iron and cook according to the manufacturer's directions. When the waffle is ready, transfer it to a rimmed baking sheet and keep warm in the oven. Repeat with the remaining batter, adding each finished waffle to the baking sheet without stacking the waffles.

Cut the waffles into sticks or wedges and serve them with the strawberry sauce for dipping.

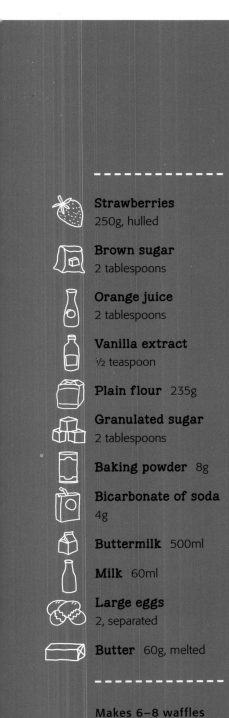

Strawberries
250g, hulled

Brown sugar
2 tablespoons

Orange juice
2 tablespoons

Vanilla extract
½ teaspoon

Plain flour 235g

Granulated sugar
2 tablespoons

Baking powder 8g

Bicarbonate of soda
4g

Buttermilk 500ml

Milk 60ml

Large eggs
2, separated

Butter 60g, melted

Makes 6–8 waffles

 Olive oil
2 tablespoons

 Small baking potatoes 2, peeled and diced

 Breakfast sausage
315g, casings removed

 Large eggs 4

 Milk 60ml

 Grated Parmesan cheese 30g

Makes 12 mini frittatas

little frittatas

Preheat the oven to 190°C.

 Line a 12-cup mini-muffin tin with paper liners.

In a large frying pan over medium heat, warm the olive oil. Add the potatoes and sauté until they begin to soften, about 5 minutes. Crumble in the sausage meat and cook, stirring often, until golden brown, about 6 minutes. Remove from the heat and transfer to a bowl to cool slightly.

 In a bowl, whisk together the eggs, milk, and cheese until blended. Stir in the cooled sausage and potatoes.

 Scoop the mixture into the lined muffin cups, dividing it evenly.

Bake until firm and doubled in size, 10–15 minutes. Let cool slightly in the pan before serving.

french toast bites with blueberry sauce

Ingredients

 Blueberries 185g

Maple syrup 180ml

Sugar 2 tablespoons

Ground cinnamon 1 teaspoon

Large eggs 2

Buttermilk 120ml

Milk 120ml

Vanilla extract 1 teaspoon

Salt Pinch

Country bread 6 thick slices, cut into 2.5cm cubes

Butter 30g

Makes 4 servings

In a small saucepan over medium-low heat, combine the blueberries and maple syrup. Bring to the boil, stirring to prevent scorching, then remove from the heat and set aside to let cool.

In a large bowl, stir together the sugar and cinnamon. Set aside.

In a large shallow bowl, whisk together the eggs, buttermilk, milk, vanilla, and salt until blended. Place the bread cubes in the egg mixture and, using a large spoon, toss gently until the cubes are evenly coated and all the egg mixture has been absorbed.

In a large frying pan over medium heat, melt half of the butter. Add half of the coated bread cubes and cook, turning often, until golden brown on all sides, about 5 minutes. Transfer the cubes to the bowl holding the cinnamon-sugar and toss to coat. Repeat with the remaining bread cubes and butter.

Divide the french toast bites into individual servings and sprinkle with the remaining cinnamon-sugar. Serve with the blueberry sauce.

Buttery and crisp on the outside, soft on the inside, French toast is perfect for many preparations. Try skewering it with fresh fruit or just sprinkling on some icing sugar. Or, use a spoonful of your favourite jam as a filling between 2 slices, then cook the toast with the filling sealed inside.

more french toast ideas

Alphabet sandwiches Have ready a whole loaf of sliced sandwich bread. Soak and cook as directed. Spread jam between 2 slices of French toast, cut into letter shapes, and sprinkle with icing sugar.

French toast skewers Give kids a handful of small skewers and bowls of French toast cubes and fresh fruit. Let them load up the skewers as they wish.

French toast soldiers Cut sandwich bread lengthwise into 12mm-wide "soldiers." Soak and cook as directed. Sprinkle with icing sugar and serve with warmed maple syrup for dipping.

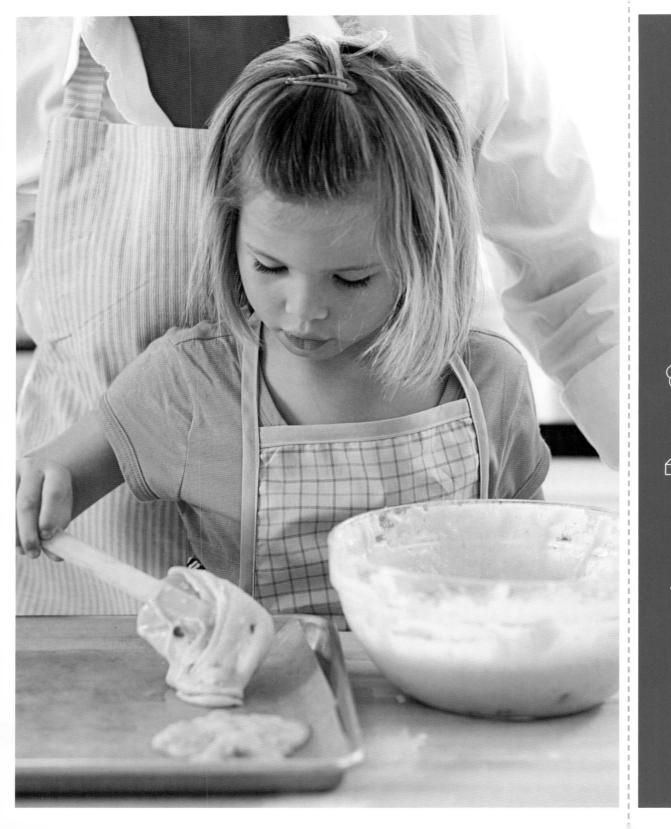

Plain flour 315g

Cornmeal 355g

Baking powder 8g

Bicarbonate of soda 2g

Salt ¼ teaspoon

Large eggs 2

Milk 160ml

Buttermilk 160ml

Butter 60g, melted

Honey 60ml, plus extra for serving

Dried cranberries 185g

Grated orange zest 1 teaspoon

Makes 24 muffins

crunchy cranberry muffin tops

Preheat the oven to 190°C. Line 2 rimmed baking sheets with baking parchment.

 In a large bowl, stir together the flour, cornmeal, baking powder, bicarbonate of soda, and salt. In a medium bowl, whisk together the eggs, milk, buttermilk, butter, and honey. Add the egg mixture to the flour mixture and stir until combined. Stir in the cranberries and orange zest and mix well.

 Drop the batter by large spoonfuls onto the prepared baking sheets, placing them well apart.

Bake until golden, about 15 minutes. Transfer to a rack to cool for 4 minutes. Serve warm with honey.

yoghurt sundaes

 In a small bowl, stir together the yoghurt, honey, and vanilla. Set aside.

 In another small bowl, combine the strawberries, mango, blueberries, blackberries, and kiwifruit. Add the orange juice and stir gently until mixed.

Have ready 2 clear glass serving dishes. Spoon one-fourth of the yoghurt mixture into each dish. Top each serving with one-fourth of the fruit mixture and then with one-fourth of the granola. Repeat the layers, ending with the granola. Serve at once, or cover and refrigerate for up to 3 hours before serving.

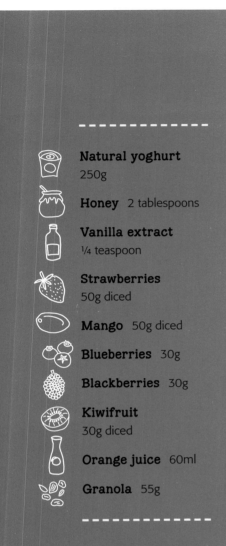

Natural yoghurt
250g

Honey 2 tablespoons

Vanilla extract
¼ teaspoon

Strawberries
50g diced

Mango 50g diced

Blueberries 30g

Blackberries 30g

Kiwifruit
30g diced

Orange juice 60ml

Granola 55g

Makes 2 sundaes

 Plain flour 155g

 Sugar 2 tablespoons

 Baking powder 8g

 Bicarbonate of soda 4g

 Salt Pinch

 Milk 250ml

 Large egg 1

 Unsalted butter 30g, melted

 Vanilla extract ¼ teaspoon

 Canola oil for greasing

 Bananas 2, sliced

 Maple syrup for serving

Makes about
24 pancakes

mini pancake stacks

Preheat the oven to 120°C.

 In a large bowl, stir together the flour, sugar, baking powder, bicarbonate of soda, and salt. In another bowl, whisk together the milk, egg, melted butter, and vanilla. Pour the milk mixture into the flour mixture and stir until smooth.

Heat a griddle pan or large frying pan, preferably nonstick, over medium heat. Lightly grease the pan with the canola oil. Using a tablespoon measure and working in batches, drop small rounds of batter onto the pan.

Cook the pancakes, turning them once with a spatula, until golden on both sides, about 3 minutes total. Transfer to a platter and keep warm in the oven. Repeat with the remaining batter, greasing the pan as needed.

 To serve, make stacks out of the pancakes. Use 3 pancakes for each stack and place banana slices in between each layer and on top. Drizzle with maple syrup and enjoy!

buttermilk scones with jam

 Plain flour 315g, plus extra for sprinkling

 Brown sugar 2 tablespoons, firmly packed

 Baking powder 8g

 Bicarbonate of soda 2g

 Salt Pinch

 Butter 90g cold, cut into small pieces, plus extra for serving

 Buttermilk 180ml

Apricot jam 75g

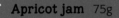

Makes about 12 scones

Preheat the oven to 230°C. Line a rimmed baking sheet with baking parchment.

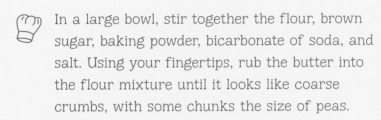 In a large bowl, stir together the flour, brown sugar, baking powder, bicarbonate of soda, and salt. Using your fingertips, rub the butter into the flour mixture until it looks like coarse crumbs, with some chunks the size of peas.

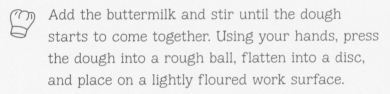 Add the buttermilk and stir until the dough starts to come together. Using your hands, press the dough into a rough ball, flatten into a disc, and place on a lightly floured work surface.

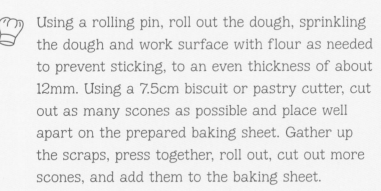 Using a rolling pin, roll out the dough, sprinkling the dough and work surface with flour as needed to prevent sticking, to an even thickness of about 12mm. Using a 7.5cm biscuit or pastry cutter, cut out as many scones as possible and place well apart on the prepared baking sheet. Gather up the scraps, press together, roll out, cut out more scones, and add them to the baking sheet.

Bake until golden, 12–15 minutes. Transfer to a rack and let cool briefly. Serve warm with butter and apricot jam.

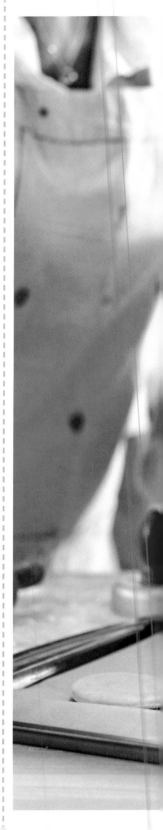

Savoury or sweet, plain or dressed up, flaky buttermilk scones are a favourite breakfast staple. In fact, you're just as likely to enjoy them served hot and fresh out of the oven alongside a generous helping of scrambled eggs and ham as spread thickly with butter and jam or drizzled with honey.

more scone ideas

Strawberry shortcake Top a scone half with an ample spoonful of cut fresh strawberries tossed with sugar, and top with a big dollop of whipped cream. Crown with the scone top to complete the shortcake.

Ham & cheese sandwich A scone is perfect for a kid-sized sandwich. Fill it with slices of Cheddar cheese and ham, artfully folded for the ideal fit. Add mustard or mayonnaise to taste.

Peach "cobbler" Sprinkle cinnamon-sugar over peach halves and roast in a 230°C oven for 10 minutes. Serve atop scone halves for a fruity open-faced treat.

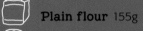**Bacon** 8 rashers, diced

Shredded Cheddar cheese 125g

Grated Parmesan cheese 30g

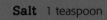**Plain flour** 155g

Salt 1 teaspoon

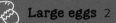**Large eggs** 2

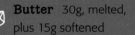**Milk** 310ml

Butter 30g, melted, plus 15g softened

Makes 12 yorkshire puddings

cheesy yorkshire puddings

Preheat the oven to 230°C.

In a frying pan over medium heat, sauté the bacon until crisp, about 8 minutes. Transfer to paper towels to drain.

In a bowl, mix together the Cheddar and Parmesan cheeses. Set aside.

In a large bowl, stir together the flour and salt. In a medium bowl, whisk together the eggs, milk, and melted butter. Pour the milk mixture into the flour mixture and stir until smooth.

Grease a 12-cup muffin tin with the softened butter. Spoon about 1 tablespoon of the bacon and 1½ tablespoons of the cheese mixture into each cup of the prepared tin.

Ladle the egg mixture into the muffin cups, dividing it evenly. Bake for 15 minutes, then reduce the oven temperature to 180°C. Make sure you do not open the oven whilst the puddings are baking or they will fall! Continue baking until the yorkshire puddings are puffed and golden, about 15 minutes longer. Transfer the puddings to a rack to cool briefly. Serve warm.

breakfast "BLT" triangles

Bacon 6 rashers

Wholemeal bread
4 slices, toasted

Butter 15g

Large eggs 2

Plum tomato
1, sliced

Salt and pepper
to taste

Makes 2 sandwiches

In a large frying pan over medium heat, cook the bacon, turning once, until crisp, about 8 minutes. Transfer to paper towels to drain briefly.

 Divide the bacon rashers evenly between 2 slices of the toasted bread.

In a nonstick frying pan over medium heat, melt the butter. One at a time, crack the eggs on the countertop and add them to the pan. Reduce the heat slightly and cook, turning once, until the whites are crisp around the edges and the yolks are firm, about 6 minutes total. Using a spatula, place the eggs on top of the bacon.

 Top each egg with tomato slices. Sprinkle the tomatoes with salt and pepper, then place a second slice of toast on top of each stack to make 2 yummy sandwiches.

Cut each sandwich into triangle quarters and serve.

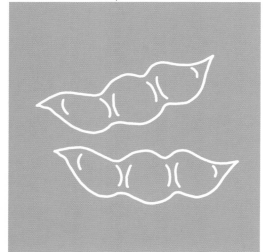

snacktime

When a quick fix is needed, or after the haze of a midmorning or afternoon nap, nothing revives more readily than a home-made, wholesome snack. Whether threading mozzarella and tomatoes on skewers, popping corn on the stovetop, or simply spreading peanut butter onto apple slices for fruit "pizzas," snacktime can provide nutritious and entertaining ideas for kids during an otherwise humdrum time of day.

Canola oil 80ml

Popcorn kernels 90g

Salt 3 teaspoons

Icing sugar 30g

Grated Parmesan cheese 120g

Butter 45g, melted

Makes 4 servings

sweet-n-salty popcorn bags

Pour the canola oil into the bottom of a large, heavy saucepan and heat over medium heat. Add the popcorn kernels, cover, and cook, shaking the pan often, until you start to hear popping. Continue to cook, shaking the pot continuously, until the popping slows to 3–5 seconds between pops. Remove from the heat and divide the popcorn evenly between 2 bowls.

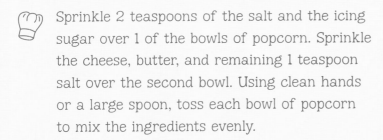 Sprinkle 2 teaspoons of the salt and the icing sugar over 1 of the bowls of popcorn. Sprinkle the cheese, butter, and remaining 1 teaspoon salt over the second bowl. Using clean hands or a large spoon, toss each bowl of popcorn to mix the ingredients evenly.

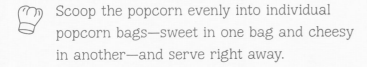 Scoop the popcorn evenly into individual popcorn bags—sweet in one bag and cheesy in another—and serve right away.

pizza kebabs

 Have ready 12 short wooden skewers. Working with 1 skewer at a time, alternately thread 2 tomatoes, 2 basil leaves, and 2 mozzarella balls onto each skewer. Or, divide the ingredients among the skewers as you like.

 Place the skewers on a serving dish and drizzle with the olive oil. Sprinkle with salt and pepper to taste and serve.

 Cherry tomatoes
1 punnet

 Small basil leaves
24

 Small mozzarella balls 24

 Olive oil 2 tablespoons

 Salt and pepper
to taste

Makes 12 kebabs

There is something about the simple act of poking stuff onto a stick that can keep kids busy for hours. Give them a set of plain wooden skewers alongside bowls filled with pieces of fresh fruit or cubes of cheese and lunch meats, and the activity becomes filled with a sense of yummy purpose and healthy sensibility.

more kebab ideas

Mixed fruit Any fruit is a good option for skewers, although fresh, seasonal choices will offer the most flavour. Try chunks of mango, kiwifruit, watermelon, cantaloupe, honeydew, or pineapple.

Strawberry cake Pair fresh strawberries or pitted cherries with bite-size cubes of vanilla or chocolate cake for a little taste of something sweet in the afternoon.

Salami & cheese If snacktime runs closer to mealtime, offer items with a bit more substance for skewering. Try cubes of salami and gruyere or ham and Cheddar.

 Red and yellow cherry tomatoes 1 punnet each

 Olive oil 2 tablespoons

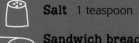 **Salt** 1 teaspoon

 Sandwich bread 8 slices

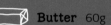 **Cheddar cheese** 8 sandwich-sized slices

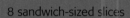 **Butter** 60g

Makes 4 servings

grilled cheese sticks with tomato soup dip

Preheat the oven to 180°C.

 Spread out the tomatoes on a rimmed baking sheet. Drizzle with the olive oil and sprinkle with the salt. Using your hands, toss the tomatoes gently to coat evenly with the oil and salt.

Bake the tomatoes until they pop open, about 15 minutes. Remove from the oven, let cool for 5 minutes, and transfer to a blender.

 Pulse the tomatoes in the blender until smooth. Then, top 4 slices of bread with 2 slices of cheese each, and cover with the remaining 4 bread slices.

Pour the tomato purée through a fine-mesh sieve set over a small saucepan, discarding the contents of the sieve. Place the saucepan over low heat and heat until hot.

Meanwhile, in a large frying pan over medium heat, melt the butter. Add the sandwiches and cook, turning once, until golden brown on both sides and the cheese has melted, about 5 minutes total.

Pour the soup into 4 small bowls. Cut each sandwich into 4 "sticks." Serve alongside the soup for dipping.

apple–peanut butter pizzas

 Golden Delicious or Granny Smith apples 2 large

 Creamy peanut butter 230g

 Flaked coconut, dried cranberries, and granola about 40g each

Makes 12–14 pizzas

Using an apple corer, core the apples. Cut each apple crosswise into 6 or 7 rounds.

 Using a small spreader, spread about 1 tablespoon of the peanut butter on each apple slice. Sprinkle the slices with the coconut, dried cranberries, and granola and serve.

 Chickpeas
1 tin (470g)

 Tahini 2 tablespoons

 Lemon juice
2 tablespoons

 Ground cumin
1½ teaspoons

 Salt 1 teaspoon

 Garlic 1 clove

 Olive oil 60ml

 Wholemeal tortillas
2 (15cm), halved

 English cucumber
1, thinly sliced

 Carrots
2, shredded

Makes 4 cones

hummous
& vegie cones

Pour the chickpeas into a sieve set over a small bowl. Measure out 60ml of the bean liquid and reserve; discard the remaining liquid.

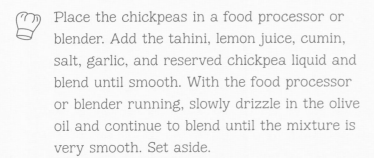 Place the chickpeas in a food processor or blender. Add the tahini, lemon juice, cumin, salt, garlic, and reserved chickpea liquid and blend until smooth. With the food processor or blender running, slowly drizzle in the olive oil and continue to blend until the mixture is very smooth. Set aside.

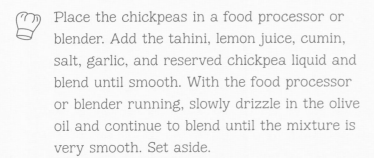 Lay the tortilla halves on a cutting board. Spread each tortilla half with an equal amount of the hummous. Cover the hummous with cucumber slices. Sprinkle the carrots evenly over the cucumber. Starting at a corner, roll up each tortilla into a cone and serve.

orange-yoghurt lollies

 Fresh orange juice
500ml

 Vanilla yoghurt
250g

Makes 4 iced lollies

In a large bowl, stir together the yoghurt and juice. Pour the mixture into 4 moulds of an iced-lolly tray, dividing it equally.

Insert an iced-lolly holder or wooden iced-lolly stick into each mould. Freeze for at least 8 hours or up to overnight.

When ready to serve, run the moulds under warm water for a few seconds to release the lollies.

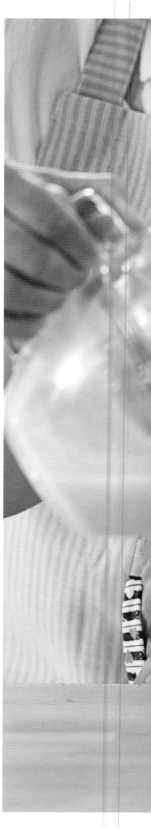

When the afternoon doldrums strike, few snacks revive kids as quickly as these fruity iced lollies. With only 2 ingredients, this recipe is easy for kids to master. They can try substituting their favourite flavours for the original, or mix and blend different fruit flavours and colours for their own unique lollies!

more yoghurt lolly ideas

Fruit juice slices Pour blended yoghurt into loaf tins before freezing, then unmould, slice, and eat with a fork. Or, leave the fruit juice out and try layering the loaf tins with different flavours of yoghurt.

Multiflavoured lollies Kids appreciate a choice when it comes to fruit flavours. Try adding grape, cherry, or mango juice as alternatives to the orange.

Fruit cups Scatter a spoonful of fresh berries over the bottom of a ramekin. Add a complementary flavour of blended yoghurt and freeze. Before serving, dip the bottom of the ramekin in warm water, then unmould.

Butter 30g, plus extra, softened for greasing

 Shredded coconut 125g

 Dried cherries 185g

 Dried blueberries 90g

 Old-fashioned rolled oats 90g

 Whole almonds 170g

 Shelled sunflower seeds 125g

 Wheat germ 80g

 Brown sugar 220g

 Honey 120ml

 Vanilla extract 1 teaspoon

 Ground cinnamon 1 teaspoon

Makes about 16 squares

granola bites

Preheat the oven to 180°C.

 Grease a 23cm square tin with the softened butter. In a large bowl, combine the coconut, cherries, and blueberries; set aside. On a rimmed baking sheet, combine the oats, almonds, sunflower seeds, and wheat germ.

Bake the oat mixture until toasted and fragrant, 5–10 minutes. Remove from the oven. Add the hot oat mixture to the fruit-coconut mixture and stir until combined.

In a saucepan over medium heat, melt the butter. Add the brown sugar, honey, vanilla, and cinnamon and stir until the sugar dissolves, about 5 minutes. Bring to the boil, then remove from the heat and pour over the fruit-oat mixture.

 Using a large spoon, gently stir together all the ingredients until well combined. Scoop the mixture into the prepared tin. Using your hands, firmly press the mixture into the tin, making a compact, even layer. The mixture will be sticky!

Let set in the pan for 10 minutes. Invert the tin onto a cutting board and lift off the tin. Cut into squares and serve.

edamame snack

In a bowl, stir together the soy sauce, sesame seeds, and sugar.

Bring a large pot of water to the boil over high heat. Add the edamame and boil for 5 minutes. Drain.

Add the beans to the soy sauce mixture. Using clean hands or a large spoon, toss gently to coat the beans with the sauce.

To eat the edamame, peel away the pod and pop the beans into your mouth! Serve warm or at room temperature.

Soy sauce
2 tablespoons

Toasted sesame seeds
2 teaspoons

Sugar ¼ teaspoon

**Frozen edamame
in their pods**
315g bag, thawed

Makes 4 servings

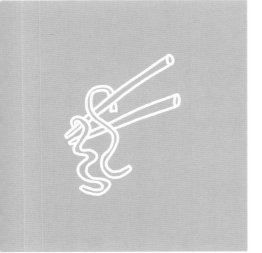

dinnertime

Kids won't need much encouragement to eat a nutritious dinner when they help make it themselves. In a kid's kitchen, pride of ownership can do more to inspire a big appetite than any amount of bargaining. Focus on menu items that include hands-on fun like ravioli, spaghetti and meatballs, tacos, and pizza. Make it interesting by letting them add all the ingredients themselves and vary them according to their own tastes.

 Large sweet potatoes
2, cut lengthwise into
sticks

 Olive oil 2 tablespoons,
plus extra for greasing

 **Salt and ground
pepper** to taste

 Minced beef 375g

 Cheddar cheese
2 slices, halved

 Small dinner rolls
4, split

 **Sliced gherkins,
ketchup, and
mustard** for serving

Makes 4 mini burgers

mini burgers with sweet potato chips

Preheat the oven to 200°C.

 Spread out the potato sticks on a rimmed baking sheet. Drizzle with the olive oil and sprinkle with salt and pepper. Using clean hands or a spatula, toss to coat evenly.

Bake until golden and crisp, 20–25 minutes. Remove from the oven and keep warm.

 Meanwhile, divide the meat into 4 equal patties, each about 12mm thick.

About 10 minutes before the chips are ready, using a basting brush, brush a heavy frying pan (preferably cast-iron) with oil and place over medium-high heat. When the pan is hot, add the patties and cook, turning once, until browned on both sides, about 6 minutes total for medium. Top each burger with a piece of cheese during the final minute of cooking.

 Put each roll, cut sides up, on a serving plate. Place a burger on the bottom half of each roll. Accompany the burgers with gherkin slices, ketchup, and mustard. Serve with the sweet potato chips alongside.

BLT salad

Preheat the oven to 200°C.

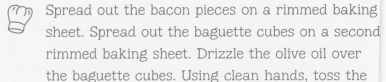 Spread out the bacon pieces on a rimmed baking sheet. Spread out the baguette cubes on a second rimmed baking sheet. Drizzle the olive oil over the baguette cubes. Using clean hands, toss the cubes to coat them evenly.

Put both baking sheets in the oven. Bake the baguette cubes until golden brown, about 10 minutes. Bake the bacon pieces until crisp, about 15 minutes.

When the baguette cubes are ready, remove them from the oven and let them cool. Then, when the bacon pieces are ready, remove them as well and transfer to paper towels to drain and cool.

To make the dressing, in a blender, combine the sour cream, lemon juice, Parmesan cheese, salt, and garlic. Blend until smooth.

In a large salad bowl, combine the lettuce, tomatoes, bacon, and baguette croutons. Drizzle with the dressing, toss to mix, and serve.

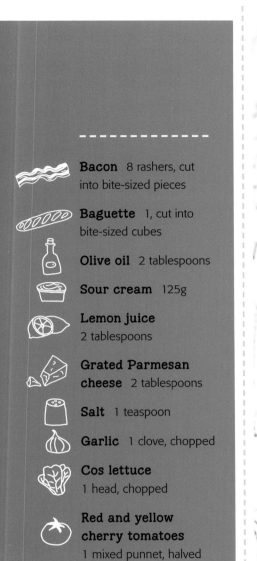

Bacon 8 rashers, cut into bite-sized pieces

Baguette 1, cut into bite-sized cubes

Olive oil 2 tablespoons

Sour cream 125g

Lemon juice 2 tablespoons

Grated Parmesan cheese 2 tablespoons

Salt 1 teaspoon

Garlic 1 clove, chopped

Cos lettuce 1 head, chopped

Red and yellow cherry tomatoes 1 mixed punnet, halved

Makes 4 servings

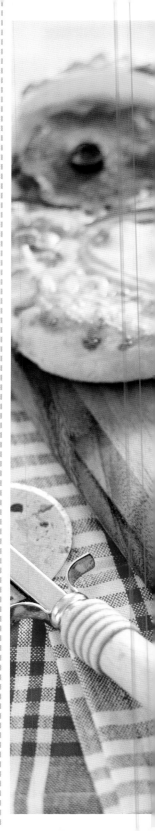

for the dough

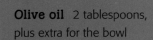
Lukewarm water
310ml

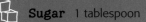
Active dried yeast
2½ level teaspoons

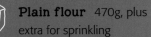
Sugar 1 tablespoon

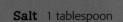
Plain flour 470g, plus
extra for sprinkling

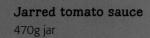
Salt 1 tablespoon

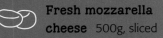
Olive oil 2 tablespoons,
plus extra for the bowl

for the toppings

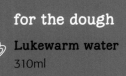
Jarred tomato sauce
470g jar

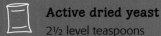
**Fresh mozzarella
cheese** 500g, sliced

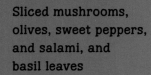
**Sliced mushrooms,
olives, sweet peppers,
and salami, and
basil leaves**

Makes 4 pizzas

pizza party

Preheat the oven to 260°C. To make the dough, pour the water into the bowl of a stand mixer, sprinkle with the yeast and sugar, and let stand until foamy, about 5 minutes. Add the flour, salt, and olive oil and beat on low speed until a rough, shaggy dough forms, about 5 minutes.

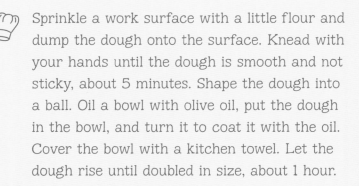

Sprinkle a work surface with a little flour and dump the dough onto the surface. Knead with your hands until the dough is smooth and not sticky, about 5 minutes. Shape the dough into a ball. Oil a bowl with olive oil, put the dough in the bowl, and turn it to coat it with the oil. Cover the bowl with a kitchen towel. Let the dough rise until doubled in size, about 1 hour.

Punch down the dough. Divide it into 4 fist-sized balls. Sprinkle a baking sheet with flour, place the balls on it, and cover with a kitchen towel. Let rise until doubled in size, about 30 minutes. Sprinkle the work surface with flour. Press each ball to deflate, then flatten and stretch it into a 25cm round. Transfer the rounds to 2 rimmed baking sheets. Spread each with tomato sauce and top with cheese and other toppings of your choice.

Bake until the cheese has melted and the crust is crisp and golden, 10–15 minutes. Cut into wedges and serve.

Whether you're making mini pizzas for a party, or a large one for a family dinner, there are all kinds of possibilities when it comes to pizza. Try folding the dough over to make a gooey calzone, slicing the dough for cheesy breadsticks, or have fun experimenting with your favourite pizza toppings.

more pizza dough ideas

Moon pie Round mozzarella slices look like moons in a red sky. The melted rounds of cheese, paired with fresh basil and tomato sauce, make up the traditional pizza Margherita, a classic kid favourite.

Calzone Sprinkle your favourite pizza ingredients over half of a dough round. Brush one edge with water, fold the dough over the ingredients, press to seal, then bake.

Cheese sticks Roll out the dough into a large rectangle, then cut it crosswise into 2.5cm strips. Sprinkle with grated Parmesan and bake in a 220ºC oven for 15 minutes.

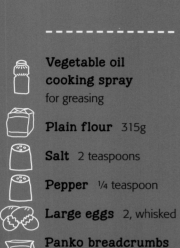

Vegetable oil cooking spray
for greasing

Plain flour 315g

Salt 2 teaspoons

Pepper ¼ teaspoon

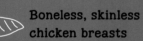**Large eggs** 2, whisked

Panko breadcrumbs 500g

Boneless, skinless chicken breasts
4, cut into 2.5cm strips

Honey 1 tablespoon

Brown sugar
1 tablespoon, firmly packed

Ketchup 80ml

Mustard 2 tablespoons

Makes 4 servings

crispy chicken bites

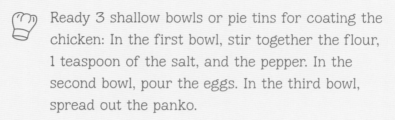

Preheat the oven to 230°C. Lightly grease a rimmed baking sheet with cooking spray.

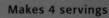 Ready 3 shallow bowls or pie tins for coating the chicken: In the first bowl, stir together the flour, 1 teaspoon of the salt, and the pepper. In the second bowl, pour the eggs. In the third bowl, spread out the panko.

Working with 1 piece at a time, dip the chicken into the flour, coating it completely and shaking off the excess; then into the egg, allowing the excess to drip off; and finally into the panko, again shaking off the excess. Lay the coated chicken pieces on the prepared baking sheet.

Bake until crisp and golden brown, about 30 minutes.

Meanwhile, make the dipping sauce. In a bowl, whisk together the honey, brown sugar, ketchup, and mustard, and the remaining 1 teaspoon salt until mixed. Transfer to individual dipping bowls.

Serve the chicken hot from the oven with the sauce.

creamy sweetcorn chowder

Working with 1 cob of sweetcorn at a time and holding it upright with the stem end down, cut straight down between the cob and the kernels, freeing the kernels. Give the cob a quarter turn after each cut. Set the kernels aside, discarding the cobs.

In a stockpot over medium heat, sauté the bacon until crisp, about 8 minutes.

 Add the sweetcorn kernels, potatoes, celery, carrot, onion, broth, and cream to the pot and stir well.

Raise the heat to high and bring to the boil. Reduce the heat to medium-low and simmer, uncovered, until the vegetables are tender, about 20 minutes. Season to taste with salt and pepper.

Ladle the chowder into soup mugs and serve hot.

 Sweetcorn 4 cobs

 Bacon 2 rashers, diced

 Small boiling potatoes 5, peeled and diced

 Celery 2 stalks, diced

 Carrot 1, peeled and diced

 Yellow onion ½, diced

 Chicken broth 1L

 Double cream 250ml

 Salt and pepper to taste

Makes 6–8 mugs of chowder

home-made fish fingers with tartar sauce

 Frozen filo dough 4 sheets, thawed

 Butter 75g, melted

 Halibut or cod fillets 250g, cut into 8 equal pieces

 Mayonnaise 125ml

 Celery ¼ stalk, finely chopped

 Gherkin relish 2 tablespoons

 Lemon juice 1 tablespoon

Salt ¼ teaspoon

Makes 8 fish fingers

Preheat the oven to 190°C. Line a rimmed baking sheet with baking parchment.

Lay 1 filo sheet on a clean work surface. Brush lightly with a little melted butter. Fold the filo in half lengthwise, and then cut in half crosswise. Cover the 2 filo pieces with a damp paper towel. Repeat with the remaining 3 sheets.

Working with 1 filo piece at a time, place it with a short end facing you, and brush it lightly with butter. Put a piece of fish on the bottom third of the filo, positioning it parallel to the bottom edge. Fold in the long sides and then roll up the filo to enclose the fish. Brush the seam lightly with butter to secure. Insert a wooden iced-lolly stick into one end of the packet. Repeat to make 8 packets.

 Arrange the fish fingers, seam side down, on the prepared baking sheet.

Bake until golden brown, 15–20 minutes.

 Meanwhile, make the tartar sauce. In a bowl, whisk together the mayonnaise, celery, relish, lemon juice, and salt. Serve the tartar sauce alongside the fish fingers.

classic beef tacos

Canola oil
1 tablespoon plus 60ml

Yellow onion
¼, chopped

Garlic 1 clove,
finely chopped

Minced beef 500g

Ground cumin
1 teaspoon

Sweet paprika
2 teaspoons

Chili powder
2 teaspoons

Salt and pepper
1 teaspoon each

Corn tortillas
6 (15cm)

**Shredded lettuce,
diced plum tomatoes,
diced avocado, and
shredded Cheddar
cheese** for serving

Makes 6 tacos

In a sauté pan over medium heat, warm the 1 tablespoon oil. Add the onion and garlic and sauté until softened, about 5 minutes. Add the minced beef and cook, stirring to break up the meat, until browned, 8–10 minutes. Drain and discard all but 1 tablespoon of the fat. Add the cumin, paprika, chili powder, salt, and pepper to the beef and stir until combined. Add 60ml water to the pan and bring to the simmer. Reduce the heat to low and let simmer, partially covered, until most of the water is absorbed, about 10 minutes. Remove from the heat and keep warm.

In another sauté pan over medium heat, warm the 60ml oil. Working with 1 tortilla at a time and using tongs, carefully slip the tortilla into the hot oil and cook, turning once, until lightly browned on both sides, about 3 minutes total. Transfer to paper towels to drain. Let cool slightly.

When the tortillas are cool enough to handle, top each one with the beef mixture, dividing evenly. Then sprinkle each one with equal amounts of lettuce, tomatoes, avocado, and cheese.

Fold each taco in half and serve right away.

It's hard to go wrong with tortillas, spiced beef mince, beans, and cheese. And there are all kinds of different ways to use these yummy ingredients. You can roll them up in flour tortillas to make burritos, or sprinkle them onto tortilla chips along with lettuce and sour cream for bite-size tostadas.

more taco ideas

Seven-layer dip In a glass bowl, layer refried beans, taco meat, sour cream, shredded lettuce, Cheddar cheese, diced tomato, and cubed avocado. Use crisp tortilla chips for scooping down to the bottom.

Nachos Arrange tortilla chips on an ovenproof plate. Top with taco meat and plenty of shredded Cheddar cheese. Broil until melted, then sprinkle with toppings like tomatoes and avocado.

Taco salad Fill a salad bowl with shredded lettuce. Top with taco meat, whole black beans, diced tomato and avocado, crushed tortilla chips, and fresh salsa.

chicken chow mein

 To make the sauce, in a liquid measuring jug, whisk together the soy sauce, 60ml water, rice vinegar, peanut oil, and cornflour. Set aside.

Bring a large pot of water to the boil over high heat. Add the noodles and cook until al dente, 5 minutes. Drain.

In a large sauté pan or wok over high heat, warm the oil. Add the chicken and cook, stirring, until browned, about 5 minutes. Remove from the pan and set aside.

Add the mushrooms, pak choi, baby corn, snap peas, and bean sprouts to the pan. Cook, stirring constantly, until softened, about 5 minutes. Drizzle the soy sauce mixture over the vegetables and cook, stirring, until the sauce has thickened, about 5 minutes. Return the cooked chicken to the pan, add the noodles, and toss to mix.

 Soy sauce 60ml

 Rice vinegar
2 teaspoons

 Peanut oil
1 teaspoon

 Cornflour
1 teaspoon

 Fresh Chinese egg noodles 500g

 Canola oil
2 tablespoons

 Boneless, skinless chicken breasts
2, diced

 Small shiitake mushrooms
250g, halved

 Baby pak choi
3 heads, chopped

 Baby corn spears
1 tin (470g), rinsed and drained

 Snap peas 250g

 Bean sprouts 100g

Makes 6 servings

spaghetti & meatballs

In a saucepan over medium heat, warm 2 tablespoons of the olive oil. Add the onion and garlic and sauté until the onion is soft, about 5 minutes. Add the tomato purée, chopped tomatoes, tomato paste, 1 tablespoon of the oregano, and the sugar. Bring to the simmer and cook until thickened, about 20 minutes.

 Meanwhile, make the meatballs. In a large bowl, combine the turkey, breadcrumbs, 60g of the Parmesan, eggs, and the remaining 1 tablespoon oregano. Season with salt and pepper. Using clean hands, mix together. Scoop out tablespoon-sized portions of the mixture, rolling each one between your palms to make small balls.

In a large sauté pan, heat the remaining 1 tablespoon oil. Working in batches, add the meatballs and cook, turning as needed, until browned on all sides, about 8 minutes. Add the browned meatballs to the tomato sauce and simmer over low heat until the meatballs are cooked through, about 20 minutes.

While the meatballs simmer, bring a large pot of salted water to the boil over high heat. Add the spaghetti, stir well, and cook until al dente, about 8 minutes or according to the package directions. Drain and transfer to warmed serving bowls. Pour the sauce and meatballs over the top, toss gently, sprinkle with remaining Parmesan, and serve.

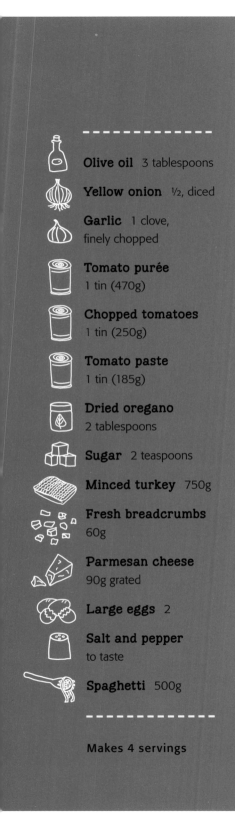

Olive oil 3 tablespoons

Yellow onion ½, diced

Garlic 1 clove, finely chopped

Tomato purée 1 tin (470g)

Chopped tomatoes 1 tin (250g)

Tomato paste 1 tin (185g)

Dried oregano 2 tablespoons

Sugar 2 teaspoons

Minced turkey 750g

Fresh breadcrumbs 60g

Parmesan cheese 90g grated

Large eggs 2

Salt and pepper to taste

Spaghetti 500g

Makes 4 servings

 Olive oil 3 tablespoons

 Chicken 500g, diced

 Yellow onion ½, chopped

 Carrots 2, chopped

 Small baking potatoes 2, peeled and diced

 Flour 25g

 Chicken broth 1L

 Salt and pepper to taste

 Double cream 125ml

 Frozen green peas 155g

 Frozen puff pastry 1 sheet, thawed

 Butter 30g, melted

Makes 6 potpies

chicken potpies

Preheat the oven to 180°C. In a large pot over medium heat, warm 2 tablespoons of the oil. Add the chicken and cook, stirring, until browned on all sides. Transfer to a plate and set aside.

Add the remaining 1 tablespoon oil to the pan. Add the onion and cook until translucent, about 4 minutes. Add the carrots and potatoes and cook, stirring frequently, until they begin to soften, 5–6 minutes. Add the flour and stir to coat the vegetables evenly. Add the chicken broth, bring to the boil, and cook until the vegetables are tender and the mixture has thickened, about 5 minutes. Season generously with salt and pepper. Stir in the cream, the reserved chicken, and the peas. Stir until just heated through. Set aside to cool.

 Meanwhile, on a floured surface, roll out the puff pastry into a large rectangle. Using a 7.5cm round pastry or biscuit cutter, cut out 6 rounds. Using a small biscuit or pastry cutter, cut out a hole in the top of each round.

 Ladle the chicken mixture into six 250ml ovenproof dishes. Top with the pastry rounds, pinching around the edge to secure. Brush the tops with the melted butter.

Bake the potpies until the crust is puffed and golden, 20–25 minutes. Let cool slightly before serving.

cheese ravioli with cherry tomatoes

 Part-skim ricotta cheese 250g

 Grated Parmesan cheese 30g, plus extra for sprinkling

 Basil leaves 2 large, finely chopped, plus extra for garnish

 Salt ½ teaspoon

 Cherry tomatoes 1 punnet, halved

Olive oil 2 tablespoons

Wonton wrappers 24

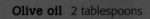

Makes 4–6 servings

 In a small bowl, stir together the ricotta cheese, Parmesan cheese, basil, and salt. Set aside.

In a sauté pan over medium heat, combine the cherry tomatoes and olive oil. Cook, stirring occasionally, just until the tomatoes begin to soften and break down, about 8 minutes. Meanwhile, bring a large pot of water to the boil over high heat.

 To make the ravioli, fill a small bowl with water and set aside for sealing the ravioli. Lay the wonton wrappers on a clean work surface. Scoop 1 teaspoon of the cheese filling onto half of each wrapper. Dip your fingertip into the water and gently rub along the outer edge of a wonton wrapper. Fold the wrapper in half and seal by gently pressing along the edge. Repeat to dampen, fold, and seal the remaining ravioli.

Carefully slip the ravioli into the boiling water and cook just until the wrappers are transparent, about 3 minutes. Using a slotted spoon, transfer the ravioli to individual serving bowls, dividing them equally. Top each serving with a spoonful of the tomatoes, sprinkle with the remaining Parmesan cheese and basil, and serve.

sweets

Considering the gooey icings, chocolate dipping, biscuit cutting, batter swirling, and multitude of sparkly sugary sprinkles, it's no wonder kids love making sweets. With all these deliciously tempting ingredients to choose from, it's nearly impossible to make a mistake. Keep recipes simple, encourage a little freedom of expression, and you'll create a cooking experience that your young ones will relish for many years to come.

inside-out apple crisp

Using an apple corer, core the apples and set aside.

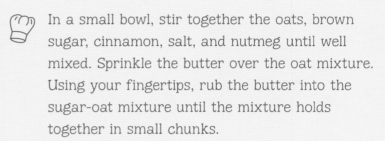 In a small bowl, stir together the oats, brown sugar, cinnamon, salt, and nutmeg until well mixed. Sprinkle the butter over the oat mixture. Using your fingertips, rub the butter into the sugar-oat mixture until the mixture holds together in small chunks.

Stuff an equal amount of the oat mixture into the centre of each apple. Stand the apples upright in a baking tin just large enough to hold them. Pour the apple juice into the bottom of the tin.

Bake until golden and tender when pierced with a knife, about 35 minutes. Transfer the apples to individual serving bowls and serve warm.

Baking apples, such as Gala or Golden Delicious 4 large

Old-fashioned rolled oats 45g

Brown sugar 185g

Ground cinnamon 1 teaspoon

Salt ¼ teaspoon

Ground nutmeg ¼ teaspoon

Butter 125g, cut into small cubes

Apple juice 120ml

Makes 4 servings

 Butter 185g

 Plain chocolate 250g, chopped

 Large eggs 4

 Vanilla extract 1 teaspoon

 Sugar 250g

 Plain flour 155g

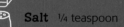 **Salt** ¼ teaspoon

 Creamy peanut butter 155g

 Chocolate chips 135g

Makes about
16 brownies

chocolate–peanut butter brownies

Preheat the oven to 180°C. Line a 23cm square baking tin with baking parchment.

Combine the butter and chocolate in a heatproof bowl and place over (not touching) barely simmering water in a saucepan. Heat, stirring frequently, until melted and smooth, about 5 minutes. Remove from the heat and let cool slightly.

 Break the eggs into a bowl. Using an electric mixer on medium speed, beat the eggs until light in colour, about 4 minutes. Beat in the vanilla and sugar until well combined, then gradually stir in the cooled chocolate until blended. Using a rubber spatula, fold in the flour and salt until evenly combined.

 Scoop the chocolate mixture into the prepared baking tin and smooth the top with the spatula. Using a tablespoon, drop 6 tablespoon-size dollops of peanut butter evenly over the top. Sprinkle with the chocolate chips.

Bake until a toothpick inserted into the centre comes out clean, 25–30 minutes. Transfer to a wire rack and let cool completely. Cut into squares and serve.

strawberry puddings

Pour 60ml water into a small bowl, sprinkle with the gelatin, and stir to combine. Let stand for 5 minutes to soften.

In a saucepan over medium heat, stir together the milk, icing sugar, and vanilla bean. Bring to the simmer for 5 minutes. Add the gelatin mixture and stir until dissolved. Remove from heat and let cool. When the milk mixture has cooled, remove the vanilla bean and discard.

Add the buttermilk and half of the diced strawberries to the milk mixture and stir together until combined.

Divide the strawberry mixture evenly among 4–6 small glasses, filling them to within about 12mm of the rim. Cover and refrigerate the glasses and the remaining strawberries until the puddings are set, at least 3 hours or up to 2 days.

Spoon the reserved chilled strawberries over the puddings and serve cold.

- **Powdered gelatin** 3 level teaspoons
- **Milk** 155g
- **Icing sugar** 90g
- **Vanilla bean** 1, split
- **Buttermilk** 620ml
- **Strawberries** 250g, hulled and diced

Makes 4–6 puddings

snowball cupcakes

Ingredients

 Granulated sugar 375g

 Butter 185g plus 1 tablespoon, softened

 Large eggs 3

 Milk 180ml

 Vanilla extract 1 tablespoon plus 1 teaspoon

 Plain flour 440g

 Cornflour 2 tablespoons

 Baking powder 12g

 Salt ⅛ teaspoon

 Cream cheese 250g

 Icing sugar 250g

  Shredded coconut 250g

Makes 24 cupcakes

Method

Preheat the oven to 180°C.

 Line two 12-cup muffin tins with paper liners. In a large bowl, using an electric mixer on medium speed, beat together the granulated sugar and the 185g butter until creamy. Add the eggs, one at time, beating well after each addition. Add the milk, 120ml water, and the 1 tablespoon vanilla and beat until combined.

 In a bowl, stir together the flour, cornflour, baking powder, and salt. With the mixer on low speed, gradually add the flour mixture to the egg mixture, beating until smooth. Divide the batter among the prepared muffin cups, filling them about two-thirds full.

Bake until a toothpick inserted in the centre comes out clean, 35–40 minutes. Let cool on a wire rack for 5 minutes, then remove the cupcakes from the tin and let cool completely.

To make the icing, in a large bowl, whisk together the cream cheese, the 1 tablespoon butter, and the 1 teaspoon vanilla. Add the icing sugar and stir until smooth.

 Generously spread icing on each cupcake, sprinkle with the shredded coconut, and eat!

Cupcakes are a classic party favourite and kids love to decorate their own. Set out plain cupcakes with bowls of icing and a range of toppings, and the celebration will swing into gear before the first one is finished. Make sure each child has two to decorate, one to enjoy at the party and one to show off at home.

more cupcake ideas

Decorations Cupcake decorating contests are a great way to get kids into the spirit of decorating. Try having a face-making contest, or encourage decorating with a theme such as flowers, bugs, cars, or zoo animals. The more theme-appropriate toppings and sprinkles you offer, the more excitement you will create.

Coloured icings Adding a few drops of food colouring to plain white icing makes for more colourful fun. Try spooning two colours of icing onto a cupcake top and swirling them together. Or, ice the cupcake with one colour and then drizzle with another colour.

 Plain flour
375g, plus more
for dusting

 Baking powder 1g

 Salt ⅛ teaspoon

 Butter 250g
(2 sticks), softened

 Granulated sugar
155g

 Large egg 1

 Vanilla extract
1½ teaspoons

 Icing sugar 125g

 Lemon juice
1 tablespoon plus
1 teaspoon

  Food colouring
2–3 drops of your
favourite colour

Makes about
12 biscuit flowers

biscuit flower lollies

In a bowl, stir together the flour, baking powder, and salt.
Set aside. In a bowl, using an electric mixer on medium
speed, beat the butter and sugar until fluffy and light,
about 5 minutes. Add the egg and vanilla and beat until
well combined. With the mixer on low speed, gradually
add the flour mixture and beat just until blended.

Press the dough into 2 flat discs, wrap in cling
film, and refrigerate until firm, about 1 hour.

Preheat the oven to 180°C.

On a lightly floured work surface, roll out
each dough disc into a 6mm-thick round. Using
flower-shaped biscuit cutters, cut out shapes
and place on 2 rimmed baking sheets. Insert
a wooden iced-lolly stick into each flower.

Bake until golden, 15–20 minutes. Let cool briefly on
the sheet, then transfer to wire racks and let cool.

To make the icing, in a small bowl, stir together
the icing sugar, lemon juice, and food colouring
until smooth. Decorate the cooled biscuits with
the icing and enjoy!

Sugar biscuit dough easily plays host to a range of possibilities. You can sandwich biscuits with fillings of melted chocolate, peanut butter, or jam. Use a small biscuit cutter to create a window in the top biscuit before baking, if you like. Or, try dipping plain or filled biscuits in melted chocolate.

more biscuit ideas

Ice cream sandwiches Set out your favourite ice cream at room temperature to soften. Spoon onto a biscuit, sandwiching another biscuit on top. Freeze until the ice cream is firm.

Jam thumbprints Roll dough into small balls. Using your thumb, make an impression in each of the balls and bake. Once cooled, fill each biscuit with jam.

Chocolate-dipped biscuits Using a double boiler, melt 250g of plain chocolate. Once the biscuits are cool, dip half the biscuit in the chocolate, place on a rack, and let the chocolate set before serving.

lemony berry bars

 Butter 125g, softened, plus more for greasing

 Plain flour 200g

 Icing sugar 30g

 Ice water 1 tablespoon

 Vanilla extract 1 teaspoon

  Salt ¾ teaspoon

 Raspberry or other berry jam 230g

 Large eggs 6

 Granulated sugar 500g

 Lemon juice 180ml

Baking powder 3g

Makes about 16 bars

Preheat the oven to 180°C. Grease a 23cm square tin.

To make the crust, in a bowl, using an electric mixer on medium speed, beat the butter until creamy. With the mixer on low speed, add 155g of the flour, the icing sugar, ice water, vanilla, and ½ teaspoon of the salt and beat just until the mixture forms a ball.

 Using clean hands, scoop the dough into the prepared tin and press to form an even layer over the tin bottom. Refrigerate for 10 minutes.

Bake the crust until golden and firm, about 15 minutes. Let cool completely on a rack. Reduce the oven temperature to 165°C.

 Using a rubber spatula, spread the jam evenly over the crust. In a bowl, combine the eggs, granulated sugar, lemon juice, the baking powder, the remaining 45g flour, and the remaining ¼ teaspoon salt. Whisk until smooth. Pour the egg mixture over the crust, spreading it with the back of the spatula to form an even layer.

Return the tin to the oven and bake until the top is set, 20–25 minutes. Let cool completely on a rack. Cut into bars or squares and serve.

 Frozen puff pastry
1 sheet, thawed

 Pitted cherries or blueberries 250g

 Sugar 45g

 Grated lemon zest
½ teaspoon

 Lemon juice
2 teaspoons plus
1 tablespoon

 Ground cinnamon
⅛ teaspoon (optional)

 Large egg 1,
lightly beaten

Icing sugar 60g

Orange juice
1 tablespoon

Makes 9 turnovers

fruity turnovers

Preheat the oven to 180°C. Line a baking sheet with baking parchment.

Place the pastry on a clean work surface. Using a rolling pin, roll out the pastry until it is a square that is 3mm thick.

Cut the pastry lengthwise into 3 equal pieces, then cut the pieces crosswise to make a total of 9 squares. Place the squares on the prepared baking sheet and set aside.

In a bowl, combine the fruit, sugar, lemon zest, 2 teaspoons lemon juice, and cinnamon, if using. Divide the fruit mixture evenly among the pastry squares, placing it in the centre of each square. Brush the edges of each square with the beaten egg. Fold the squares on the diagonal to enclose the filling, and press along the edge with a fork to seal in the filling.

Bake until golden brown, about 15 minutes. Transfer the turnovers to a rack to cool completely.

Meanwhile, make the glaze. In a bowl, whisk together the icing sugar, orange juice, and remaining 1 tablespoon lemon juice. Drizzle the glaze over the cooled turnovers and serve.

ice cream bonbons

Line a baking sheet with greaseproof paper. Using a 5cm ice cream scoop, scoop out 20 balls of ice cream, placing the balls on the prepared baking sheet. Have ready 20 small wooden cocktail picks.

 Poke a cocktail pick into each ice cream ball and place the baking sheet in the freezer until the balls are firm, 30–60 minutes. Meanwhile, set out several small bowls of your favourite topping ingredients.

Combine the chocolate and oil in a heatproof bowl and place over (not touching) barely simmering water in a saucepan. Heat, stirring frequently, until melted and smooth, about 5 minutes. Remove the bowl from the heat and let cool slightly.

 Dip the frozen ice cream balls into the melted chocolate, letting the excess drip back into the bowl, then dip into a topping ingredient. Place each bonbon back on the lined baking sheet. Return the baking sheet to the freezer and freeze until the chocolate hardens, about 30 minutes. Serve the bonbons in a bowl, with the picks up.

Favourite ice cream
1 container

Bonbon toppings
such as shredded
coconut and chopped
peanuts

Dark chocolate
345g, grated

Canola oil
2 tablespoons

Makes 20 bonbons

The many uses for chocolate-covered ice cream balls is a topic most kids would love to explore. You can dip the bonbons into all kinds of toppings, from chocolate sprinkles to toasted nuts to small candies. Let your imagination go wild, with more fanciful puddings like banana splits, bonbon kebabs, or a bonbon "cake."

more bonbon ideas

Banana split Nestle two bonbons between slices of fresh banana and a dollop of cherry-topped whipped cream. Use a spoon to break through the bonbons' hard chocolate shells, and enjoy!

Bonbon skewers Thread bonbons onto skewers, alternating them with fresh or frozen strawberries, raspberries, or banana slices.

Ice cream cake Arrange bonbons around the perimeter of your favourite cake as a decoration. When the cake is cut, everyone gets a bonbon or two with their slice for an instant cake and ice cream dessert.

waffle iron

An electric, countertop appliance used to make waffles. Comes in different sizes and shapes, like round, square, and Belgian.

griddle

A flat, rectangular cooking surface—ideal for pancakes or French toast—which can be used over one or two cooker rings.

biscuit cutter

Metal cutters—in all different shapes and sizes—tend to be the best as they hold their shape and cut through dough easily.

large grater/shredder

A metal kitchen tool that makes it easy to shred cheese or grate citrus zest.

small sieve

A mesh bowl, either fine or coarse, that is used for draining liquids or making dry ingredients smooth and powdery.

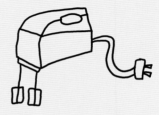

electric mixer

A handheld mixer with different speeds that quickly whips egg whites or beats batters and doughs.

whisk

A balloon-shaped tool used to whip together liquid ingredients and batters for even consistency.

ladle

A long-handled spoon with a deep bowl that is used to serve soups or stews.

wooden spoon

A long-handled wooden spoon is the best choice for stirring foods whilst they cook, as it will not scratch the pan.

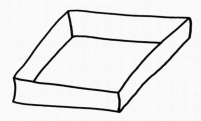

square tins

Metal baking tins, lined with baking parchment or aluminium foil, are great for baking brownies or bars.

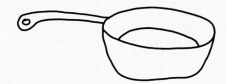
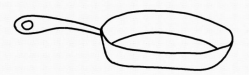

saucepans with lids

Deep pans that come in different sizes are used for stovetop cooking such as boiling pasta or simmering sauce.

frying pans

Shallow pans used on the stovetop for frying or cooking all kinds of food. The most common size is a 25cm pan.

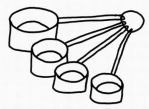

measuring cups

Straight-rimmed cups used for measuring dry ingredients. The straight sides make it easy to level off ingredients.

measuring spoons

A set of spoons, usually from ¼ teaspoon to 1 tablespoon, used to measure small amounts of dry or liquid ingredients.

liquid measuring jug

Jugs used to measure liquids are clear glass or plastic so you can line up the amount of liquid with the correct marking on the side.

spatula

A wide, flat tool with thin edges that is used for slipping under food to flip or turn during cooking.

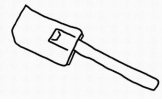

rubber spatula

A flexible rubber tool with a handle that is used to scrape the sides of mixing bowls and fold ingredients together.

rolling pin

A wooden or plastic tool used to roll out dough. Rolling pins with handles on each end are usually easier to use.

glossary

This list of common cooking terms and ingredients will help you when you are cooking the recipes in this cookery book.

bake

To cook items such as breads and pastries in an oven using hot, dry air.

baking powder

This chemical leavener is used to make baked goods like breads and muffins rise. It is made of bicarbonate of soda, an acid such as cream of tartar, and cornflour or flour. If your recipe calls for baking powder, you can substitute bicarbonate of soda, an equal amount of cornflour, and twice the amount of cream of tartar.

beat

To mix ingredients vigorously with a spoon, fork, or the beaters on an electric mixer.

bicarbonate of soda

Like baking powder, this is also a chemical leavener used to make baked goods rise. It is also known as baking soda. Bicarbonate of soda is commonly combined with an acidic ingredient like buttermilk or lemon juice to activate it. You cannot use baking powder as a replacement for bicarbonate of soda.

blend

To combine two or more ingredients thoroughly. Also, to use an electric blender to mix ingredients.

boil

To heat a liquid until bubbles constantly rise to its surface and break. A gentle boil is when small bubbles rise and break slowly. A rapid boil is when large bubbles rise and break quickly.

buttermilk

A cultured milk, often lowfat, that has a thickened texture and tangy flavour. It is delicious in baked goods like scones.

chill

To place an item in the refrigerator until it is cold all the way through. Chilling helps to firm up or set some dishes, like puddings.

chocolate

Chocolate is available in many different forms, including plain chocolate; dark chocolate sold as blocks, bars, and chips; and unsweetened chocolate (solid chocolate that has no added milk or sugar which is sold in small squares and often used for baking). Unsweetened cocoa powder—which is not the same as hot cocoa mix—is a fine chocolate powder that is often used for baking.

chop

To cut food into evenly sized pieces. Finely chopped pieces are small; coarsely chopped pieces are large.

cinnamon

A sweet, brown spice made from grinding the bark of the tropical evergreen tree.

coat

To cover the surface of a pan or baking dish or an ingredient like chicken with butter, oil, flour, crumbs, or another ingredient.

cobbler

A deep-dish fruit dish topped with a crumbled sconelike topping, sprinkled with sugar, and baked until bubbly.

coconut (packaged)

A firm, white fruit that is available flaked or shredded, sweetened or unsweetened.

consistency

How thick or thin, fine or coarse, smooth or lumpy an ingredient or mixture of ingredients is.

cornmeal

Flour that is ground from dried sweetcorn kernels. It may be finely or coarsely ground. Stone-ground cornmeal is preferred by many because it contains the germ of the maize, giving it more texture and making it more flavourful and nutritious.

cream cheese

A soft, creamy, spreadable cheese made from cow's milk. It has a mildly tangy flavour and is often used in cheesecake.

cream, whipping

Cream is what rises to the top of milk. It's very rich and contains a lot of fat, up to 50 percent. You can also use double cream to make a richer whipped cream.

disc

A flat round shape. Dough is often formed into discs before rolling out and for easy storage in the refrigerator or freezer.

dissolve

To mix a fine-textured, solid ingredient, such as sugar or salt, into a liquid, such as water, until the solid disappears.

divide

To split ingredients or a batch of dough or batter into smaller, usually equal, quantities.

dollop

A heaping spoonful of an ingredient such as whipped cream or sour cream that is used to garnish food like soup, tacos, or pie.

drain

To pour off liquid, leaving the solids behind. To do this, the solids and liquid are usually poured into a strainer or colander.

drizzle

To pour an ingredient like icing or lemon juice over food in a thin stream.

dust

To cover a food, your hands, or a work surface lightly with a powdery substance such as flour or icing sugar.

edamame

The Japanese name for green soy beans. Often served in their pods, sprinkled with salt. To eat, pop the beans out of the pod.

eggs

Sold in a range of sizes, from small to large. The recipes in this book use large-sized eggs. Look for organic, free-range eggs for the best quality.

flour, plain

The most common type of flour available, plain flour is made from a blend of wheats that make it equally reliable for muffins, cakes, biscuits, and other baked goods.

garnish

To decorate a dish before serving. Also, the food used to decorate a dish. For example, you can garnish a bowl of soup with a dollop of sour cream or a sprinkle of fresh herbs.

gelatin

A thickener which helps dishes such as jelly, moulded puddings, and marshmallows keep their shape.

granola

A breakfast food or snack made from a mixture of grains, nuts, and dried fruits.

grate

To cut an ingredient, such as Parmesan, into very fine pieces on the surface of very small, sharp-edged holes on a grater/shredder.

grease

To rub a tin or baking dish with butter or oil to prevent sticking. Another way to prevent sticking is to line a tin with baking parchment cut to fit the tin.

heat (cooker)

A recipe should tell you the heat level to use on the cooker. Heat levels are marked on the dial for each cooker ring. Low heat is usually just above the lowest setting, which recipes sometimes call very low. Medium heat is when the dial is turned on halfway. High heat comes when the dial is at its highest setting. Medium-low and medium-high heats are midway between settings.

heatproof

Dishes that can be used in the oven or on top of a cooker.

hummous

A spread made from chickpeas, tahini, lemon juice, garlic, and olive oil.

icing

A sweet mixture that is used to fill and top cakes, cupcakes, and biscuits. It can be flavoured with vanilla, chocolate, lemon, or other flavours.

invert

To turn a pan upside down so that the food falls gently onto a cooling rack or a dish.

jam

A sweet, chunky preserve containing the edible portion of the fruit in its entirety.

kebab

Pieces of meat, seafood, vegetables, or fruits served on a wooden or metal skewer. Kebabs are often marinated and barbecued.

knead
To work a yeasted dough with your hands or a mixer, using pressing, folding, and turning motions. When dough is fully kneaded, it becomes smooth and elastic.

lengthwise
In the same direction as, or parallel to, the longest side of a piece of food or a pan or dish. This term is often used in directions for serving or cutting.

line
To cover the inside of a tin with aluminium foil, greaseproof paper, or baking parchment to prevent food from sticking.

maple syrup
Pure maple syrup is made from the boiled sap of the sugar maple tree. For the best flavour look for pure maple syrup rather than what's known as "pancake syrup," which is often made from corn syrup.

melt
To heat a solid substance, such as butter or chocolate, just until it becomes smooth and liquid.

mix
To stir together dry or wet ingredients until they are combined. When a recipe warns you not to overmix, you should stir just until the ingredients are combined without streaks, and then stop. Too much stirring can release tiny air bubbles and make a batter deflate.

mound
To heap ingredients into a raised mass.

muffin
A cup-shaped quick bread that can either be savoury, such as cornmeal, or sweet, such as blueberry or chocolate.

nutmeg
The hard seed of the nutmeg tree. This fragrant spice is grated or ground and most often used in sweets like rice pudding.

panko
Dried, Japanese-style breadcrumbs, which cook up extra crispy when used to coat ingredients like chicken or prawns.

peanut butter
Made from ground peanuts, this spreadable "butter" is used for sandwiches and more.

peel
To strip or cut away the skin or rind from fruits and vegetables.

pinch
The amount of a dry ingredient that you can pick up, or "pinch," between your thumb and forefinger; usually less than about ⅛ teaspoon. Often used to measure salt, pepper, and heavy spices.

preheat
To heat an oven to a specific temperature before using it.

puff pastry
A light, flaky pastry that is formed by rolling and folding dough and butter in many layers so that it expands when it is baked.

raisins
Sweet, dried grapes that are used in a variety of baked products.

reduce (heat)
To turn down the heat under a pan on the stovetop or inside the oven.

refrigerate
To place food in the refrigerator to chill, to become firm, or for storage.

rise
What happens to a dough or batter when it grows and becomes more airy as a result of a gas (carbon dioxide) released by yeast, baking powder, or bicarbonate of soda.

roll out
To flatten dough with a rolling pin until it is smooth, even, and typically thin.

room temperature
The temperature of a comfortable room. Butter or eggs are often brought to room temperature so they will blend more easily into a batter or dough.

set
When a liquid congeals and thickens or when a dough or batter becomes more solid as it cooks or cools.

set aside

To put ingredients to one side whilst you do something else.

shred

To cut an ingredient, such as carrots or cheese, on the medium or large holes of a grater/shredder.

simmer

To cook something slowly on the cooker at just below the boiling point. The surface should be steaming and nearly bubbling.

slice

To cut food lengthwise or crosswise with a knife, forming thick or thin pieces.

soften

To let an ingredient, such as butter, sit at room temperature until it is soft enough to spread or mix.

spread

To apply a soft food, such as icing or butter, over another food in an even layer.

stir

To move a spoon,fork, or whisk in a circular motion through ingredients to combine them.

sugar

The three most common sugars are: icing sugar (finely ground granulated sugar with a bit of cornflour), granulated sugar (small, white granules), and brown sugar (a moist blend of granulated sugar and treacle).

Swiss roll

A thin sheet of cake layered with jam and then rolled up. A Swiss roll tin refers to a rimmed baking sheet.

tartar sauce

A creamy, tangy sauce that is usually made from mayonnaise, capers, chopped pickled gherkins, lemon, and herbs. Often served with fish or shellfish.

thicken

When a food changes from a loose, liquid consistency to a thick, firm one. Often, this happens through simmering or chilling, or by adding a thickener such as gelatin.

tortillas, wholemeal

Flatbreads that are cooked on a griddle and made from wheat flour. They are used in Mexican cooking and can be eaten plain or wrapped around fillings such as beans, rice, and/or barbecued meats and poultry.

toss

To mix ingredients together by tumbling them in the bowl with your hands, two forks, or two spoons.

vanilla extract

A liquid flavouring made from vanilla beans, the dried pods of a type of orchid. Look for pure vanilla extract for better flavour.

whisk

To stir a liquid such as whipping cream or egg whites vigorously with a whisk, adding air and increasing its volume until fluffy.

work surface

A clean, flat space—usually in the kitchen—used for cutting, mixing, or preparing foods.

yeast, active dried

A type of fungus that makes breads and other baked goods rise. Active dried yeast comes in dried granules and is easy to use. In recent years, quick-rise yeasts have been developed to make breads rise in only half the usual time.

yoghurt

A custardlike, cultured milk product that has a tangy flavour, and can be plain or sweetened and flavoured with fruit.

zest

The thin, brightly coloured outer layer of peel of a citrus fruit. It is most often grated or cut into strips.

index

COOKING WITH KIDS

Conceived and produced by Weldon Owen Inc.

415 Jackson Street, San Francisco, CA 94111

Phone: 415 291 0100

Fax: 415 291 8841

In collaboration with Williams-Sonoma, Inc.

3250 Van Ness Avenue, San Francisco, CA 94109

A WELDON OWEN PRODUCTION

First printed in 2009

10 9 8 7 6 5 4 3 2 1

ISBN: 978 1 74089 987 1

Printed in China by Toppan-Leefung Printing Limited

WELDON OWEN INC.

Executive Chairman, Weldon Owen Group   John Owen

CEO and President   Terry Newell

Senior VP, International Sales   Stuart Laurence

VP, Sales and New Business Development   Amy Kaneko

Director of Finance   Mark Perrigo

VP and Publisher   Hannah Rahill

Executive Editor   Kim Laidlaw

Editor   Lauren Hancock

VP and Creative Director   Gaye Allen

Associate Creative Director   Emma Boys

Designer and Illustrator   Diana Heom

Production Director   Chris Hemesath

Production Manager   Michelle Duggan

Color Manager   Teri Bell

Photo Manager   Meghan Hildebrand

Text Writer   Lisa Atwood

Photographer   David Matheson

Digital Technicians   Eszter Marosszeky & William Moran

Food Stylist   Erin Quon

Assistant Food Stylist   Victoria Woollard

Prop Stylist   Lauren Hunter

ACKNOWLEDGMENTS

Weldon Owen wishes to thank the following individuals for their kind assistance:
Ken DellaPenta, Leslie Evans, and Sharon Silva.

Homeowners   Lauren and Brad Hancock.

Models   Sam Blake, Sean O'Neal, Teya O'Neal, Erin Quon, Tatum Quon, Clara Tunny, Mia Turner, and Ozzy Wilson.